Good wishes for your marriage, which include the wisdom found in this small book of readings. If you set aside a time each day to read and think and talk together about the matters discussed in this book, you will enrich your marriage and nurture your shared life. The blessings will come from God, who will make these readings a significant gift to your life together.

TO: _Elizabeth and Greg_

FROM: _Meaghan and Matt_

DATE: _6/16/2012_

Happy wedding! May you have many blessed years together!

I DO

*30 Readings to Inspire Love and Conversation
About Important Issues in Marriage*

GLADYS HUNT & KEITH HUNT

DISCOVERY HOUSE
PUBLISHERS®

Discovery House Publishers is affiliated with RBC Ministries,
Grand Rapids, Michigan.

Discovery House books are distributed to the trade exclusively by
Barbour Publishing, Inc., Uhrichsville, Ohio.

Requests for permission to quote from this book should be directed to:
Permissions Department, Discovery House Publishers,
P.O. Box 3566, Grand Rapids, MI 49501.

Interior design by Sherri L. Hoffman

Library of Congress Cataloging-in-Publication Data

Hunt, Gladys M.
    I do : 30 readings to inspire love and conversation about important
issues in marriage / Gladys Hunt and Keith Hunt.
        p. cm.
    Includes bibliographical references and index.
    ISBN 978-1-57293-377-4 (alk. paper)
    1. Spouses—Prayers and devotions. 2. Marriage—Religious
aspects—Christianity--Meditations. I. Hunt, Keith. II. Title.
    BV4596.M3H87 2010
    242'.644—dc22   2010004542

Printed in the United States of America

10 11 12 13 14 / 10 9 8 7 6 5 4 3 2 1

"It is the will of God that, in marriage, husband and wife experience a lifelong unity of heart, body and mind."

METHODIST WORSHIP BOOK

Foreword

A full life is a good thing. Still it surprised us when our oldest grandson was about to marry. It seemed too soon. But even grandparents have to face the facts. The years had rolled by and one of our progeny had chosen a bride for himself, drawing us into his hopes and dreams and happiness. Our glad response was a desire to roll up all the joy in the world and give it to this shining couple whose love for each other was good and beautiful. The same thing happened when our second grandson chose a wife.

Our two grandsons, and now their wives, had woven themselves into our hearts, and we found ourselves wanting to give them the moon! Lacking *that* opportunity, we decided to share our lives in a more intentional way with them. Our marriage is fifty years old and still counting, and we have collected a bit of wisdom along the way. One of those bits is the truth found in a disclaimer by A. M. Juster:

> Despite what's promised when you marry,
> Actual results may vary.

God is a "relational" expert. He created us for relationships—a relationship with Him and with each other. Marriage is His idea. Who better, then, to tell us how to make the marriage relationship work for us? Over the years He has shown us that He is indeed the Creator of our happiness. It's all in His Book—the principles that make life meaningful and good.

For many years we worked with InterVarsity Christian Fellowship on American university campuses, challenging students to think through issues of life and its meaning, truths about God and what it means to live as a Christian. As we entered into the lives of students, inevitably we talked about sex and relationships and "finding happiness." We have lost count of how many talks we have given on this all-consuming subject to groups of students. Our grandsons had already heard their quota of teaching from us on this subject, along with that modeled by their own parents. But now they were facing the real deal for themselves.

It's true that "love is a many splendored thing." It has multiple facets. It is always more than we know. So we decided to make a collection of readings to remind our grandchildren of what love looks like in everyday life. We designed the content so that they would do three things in each reading: listen to God, talk together about what He said, and then ask for His help.

At the time of their marriage, we carefully handcrafted a book for each couple. It is like sharing our own lives to remind them of things that make life together flourish. Our hope is that they will go through the book more than once, since life keeps bringing up issues that need attention. It's truth that will never be outdated. It is our best shot at giving them "the moon."

When others saw the books, they suggested that we should share this material with other couples whose marriages would benefit from what they read in our handmade book. Thus we share it with you now in a new format. We hope as you use it that you will come to the same conclusion about its value.

GLADYS HUNT & KEITH HUNT

A cord of three strands is not quickly broken.
(ECCLESIASTES 4:12)

It takes three to make a good marriage:
husband, wife, God.

To make marriage work best,
God must be part of the relationship.

It's much like the tent illustration below:

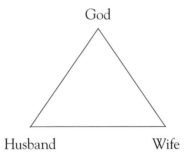

It's a simple truth: the closer you are to God,
the closer you are to each other.

C. S. Lewis called it "the intolerable compliment" this awesome offer of a relationship with God. Like Adam and Eve, our first instinct may be to hide from so terrible a friendship. Yet when we accept the offer, we find, to our astonishment, that we were made for this—to relate to the living God.

It is hard to miss how much God wants to relate to us. The more we look at the evidence, the more obvious it becomes that the world exists so that God may love us. We were made to relate to Him, and therefore our highest activity is to respond to His invitation.

That is only part of the story, however. We were also made to relate to each other. God made us "relational beings." This is what being human is all about. Ask people who are fully alive what gives life meaning, and they will tell you about their relationships.

These readings explore the dimensions of your relationship to each other and to God as you begin life together.

And remember, God speaks to us through the Scripture. It is God's Word and thus is the most important part of these readings. Read it each time as the basis for discussing the insights and comments on the passage.

Reading 1

Love is patient; love is kind.
It does not envy, it does not boast, it is not proud.
It is does not dishonor others, it is not self-seeking,
It is not easily angered, it keeps no record of wrongs.
Love does not delight in evil but rejoices with the truth.
It always protects, always trusts, always hopes,
always perseveres.
Love never fails.

1 CORINTHIANS 13:4–8

$\mathcal{W}$e drove away after the wedding and the reception feeling a kind of euphoria. The love of our families and friends, the beautiful music, the sacred vows—all of it was just as we had hoped it would be. We talked about it together and shared our happiness, and then we were silent.

We were married! It was an overwhelming truth: we were committed to love each other until death would separate us. We belonged to each other, and would soon give ourselves to each other unreservedly. The oneness that we had been developing emotionally and intellectually could now be expressed physically without reserve. We were incredibly excited about the prospect.

Yet both of us knew that the passion we felt was not the whole of love, only one wondrous expression of it. We did a wise thing that first night together. We read these verses from 1 Corinthians 13 together and then we prayed that God would make our love that strong and that good and that concerned for the other person.

It was a good way to begin. We've thought about it many times since then and realize that what we did acknowledged a great truth: *it takes three to make a good marriage.*

* Look at the verses again. Notice what love is and what it is not.

- What phrases or descriptions of love seem most important to you?
- Explain why you feel this way.
- What is the personal responsibility of each of you in keeping this standard?

Prayer: Father God, love is so awesome! Together we have felt the ecstasy of the physical, the closeness of our bodies, the warm safe caring of love. Bless us, dear Lord, lest we forget other dimensions of love that will make us into the people you want us to be. Thank you for giving us to each other. Amen.

Reading 2

When I consider your heavens,
the work of your fingers,
the moon and the stars,
which you have set in place,
what are mere mortals that you are mindful of them,
human beings that you care for them?
You made them a little lower than the heavenly beings*
    and crowned them with glory and honor.

PSALM 8:3–5

*A little less than God (RSV)

$\mathcal{H}$ow many times have you looked out at a full moon shimmering on the lake, or at a black night studded with stars, and repeated the sentiments of this psalm? Looking at the vastness of the created universe makes us feel small and insignificant. We ask with the psalmist, "Who are we that God cares so much for us?" Yet, in God's economy, we are crowned with glory and honor.

That's why C. S. Lewis writes:

"There are no *ordinary* people. You have never talked to a mere mortal. Nations, cultures, arts, civilisations—these are mortal, and their life is to ours as the life of a gnat. But it is immortals whom we joke with, work with, marry, snub, and exploit—immortal horrors or everlasting splendors. This does not mean that we are to be perpetually solemn. We must play. But our merriment must be of that kind (and it is, in fact, the merriest kind) which exists between people who have, from the outset, taken each other seriously—no flippancy, no superiority, no presumption. And our charity must be a real and costly love....

Because we are made in the image of God, says Lewis, "it is with awe... that we should conduct all our dealings

> $\mathcal{L}$OVE IS OF GOD. THAT WE CAN KNOW LOVE IS EVIDENCE THAT WE ARE MADE IN THE IMAGE OF GOD.

with one another, all friendships, all loves, all play, all politics. There are no *ordinary* people" (*The Weight of Glory*).

You are no ordinary person. You have married no ordinary person. You have married someone created by God to be an everlasting splendor! Both of you are made in the image of God.

- In what ways does this truth elevate your respect for each other?
- How do you treat someone else who is made "in the image of God?"
- What can you do to help each other remember this amazing truth?

Prayer: LORD *God, the potential each of us brings to this marriage is awesome. Whatever we are, we are in relation to you. You have made us and marked us as your special possession. Help us to remember this when we live and plan as if we were on our own. Keep us free from a self-centered life, we pray. Amen.*

Reading 3

In the beginning God created the heavens and the earth . . .

And God said, "Let there be light," and there was light . . .

And God said, "Let there be a vault between the waters to separate water from water" . . . And it was so. God called the vault "sky" . . .

And God said, "Let the water under the sky be gathered to one place, and let dry ground appear." And it was so . . . And God saw that it was good . . .

And God said, "Let there be lights in the vault of the sky to separate the day from the night" . . . And it was so . . .

And God said, "Let the water teem with living creatures, and let birds fly above the earth across the vault of the sky" . . . And God saw that it was good . . .

And God said, "Let the land produce living creatures according to their kinds" . . . And it was so . . . And God saw that it was good. Then God said, "Let us make human beings in our image, in our likeness, so that they may rule over the fish in the sea and the birds in the air, over the livestock, and all the wild animals, and over all the creatures that move along the ground.

GENESIS 1:1–26

$\mathcal{D}$id you notice the stirring rhythm that marks the unfolding of the creative work of God in these verses from Genesis 1? *And God said... Let there be... And it was so.* It has the beat of a contemporary rap, full of rhythmic repetitions. God speaks a world into being, creating all things by the word of His power.

Six times this pattern repeats itself: *And God said, "Let there be... and it was so."* God is clearly the subject of this passage. The Creator creates and furnishes a universe by His commands. No wonder "the morning stars sang together and all the angels shouted for joy" (Job 38:7).

But suddenly the pattern changes. God is about to do something new. With an economy of words our own beginning is explained. Unlike prior creation, God does not speak human beings into existence. Rather He says, *"Let us make human beings..."* and then He scoops up the dust of the earth, sculpts a human being, and breathes into his nostrils the breath of life (Genesis 2:7).

A mysterious synthesis: the dust of the earth and the life of God, the material and the spiritual. God makes a complete being: spirit, mind, and body—the likeness of God in a human being. A special production!

The Genesis account is not meant to be a detailed description of creation, but rather a strong statement about who the Creator is and His evaluation of what He has made.

It underscores our divine beginnings and gives us both a relationship and accountablilty to the One who made us. From the beginning we are special in His sight.

- What do these verses tell you about God?
- What does God mean by saying "Let us…" and "in *our* image and according to *our* likeness"?
- In what ways are you accountable to God?

Prayer: Father God, Creator of heaven and earth, the One who made us in your image, our hearts kneel in worship before your power and glory. We acknowledge your love and joy in what you created. Help us to live together with a sense of wonder at all you have given us. Amen.

Reading 4

The Lord God said, "It is not good for the man to be alone. I will make a helper suitable for him."

Now the Lord God had formed out of the ground all the wild animals and all the birds of the air. He brought them to the man to see what he would name them; and whatever the man called each living creature, that was its name. So the man gave names to all the livestock, the birds in the sky and all the wild animals.

But for Adam no suitable helper was found. So the Lord God caused the man to fall into a deep sleep; and while he was sleeping, he took one of the man's ribs and then closed up the place with flesh. Then the Lord God made a woman from the rib he had taken out of the man, and he brought her to the man. The man said,

> *"This is now bone of my bones*
> *and flesh of my flesh;*
> *she shall be called 'woman,'*
> *for she was taken out of man."*

For this reason a man will leave his father and mother and be united to his wife, and they will become one flesh.

Genesis 2:18–24

*M*arriage is God's idea. Whenever we acknowledge this, there is a stirring inside us that tells us we are in on something BIGGER than ourselves. You have just read the drama of how it came to be.

God likely had more in mind than naming animals when He paraded all living creatures before the man. What a colorful scene this exciting project must have been, and notice how seriously God took the man's contribution. Yet this significant responsibility only made Adam's "aloneness" a more painful reality. God wanted Adam to experience and acknowledge his need to be "in community" with another person of *his own kind*. (*"But for Adam no suitable helper was found!"*)

The word *helper* in Hebrew is a strong word indicating strength and capability. That same Hebrew word describes God as our *helper* in Psalm 46. In Adam's case what is needed is *a helper corresponding to the man*. There is no hierarchy here. We are born with, we are created with, a need to belong to someone who is our equal. Without this, we are innately lonely.

God made the first bride and escorted her to the man. What a wedding ceremony that must have been! The Hebrew word that describes Adam's response is like a shout of "Hurrah!" What a marvelous design: someone like him and yet different!

- What are the implications of God making woman in the way described?
- What might God's choice of a rib mean to both man and woman?
- How did Adam show his approval of the woman?
- Notice the comment on marriage that immediately follows in verse 24.

Prayer: Dear Lord, thanks for your special plan to put us together. We see your hand in our lives in many ways. We're glad this is more than just our idea of a good thing—that you have something Big in mind in bringing us to each other. Help us to learn and appreciate all it means to belong to each other. Amen.

Reading 5

For this reason a man will leave his father and mother and be united to his wife, and they will become one flesh. The man and his wife were both naked and they felt no shame.

GENESIS 2:24–25

"Haven't you read," he replied, "that at the beginning the Creator 'made them male and female', and said 'For this reason a man will leave his father and mother and be united to his wife, and the two will become one flesh'? So they are no longer two, but one. Therefore what God has joined together, let no one separate."

JESUS IN MATTHEW 19:4–6

"For this reason a man will leave his father and mother and be united to his wife, and the two will become one flesh."

PAUL IN EPHESIANS 5:31

$\mathcal{O}$ne flesh. Oneness. This is a God-idea. Human beings seem to specialize in separateness; we worry about personal rights. The world's pronouns are *I, me, mine*. We push for *self* even as we long for intimacy and belonging.

God, however, has *oneness* as the goal in marriage. That the Genesis 2 verse is repeated by Jesus (Matthew 19:5) and by Paul (Ephesians 5:31) gives you some clues as to its importance in understanding marriage.

Have you ever thought about God's own experience of oneness within the Godhead? From His earliest revelation to us (Genesis 1:26) God speaks of himself in plural form. "Let *us* make man... " That's what the Trinity is all about: one God, existing as Father, Son, and Holy Spirit. God exists "in community" in that sense. Can you imagine what kind of fellowship, what oneness of purpose, what joy in each other takes place within the Godhead?

In a less cosmic sense, God has that kind of fellowship in mind for you in marriage. You live in a body designed by God. You didn't invent sexual pleasure, and you are not the first to discover its wonders. God made sexuality. Because you are finite, limited as human beings, He made you so you could physically express "oneness"—be joined to each other to experience *oneness*.

Feel a bit of awe over that! God lets you express physically what should be happening in every other part of

31

your personalities—the blending of hearts and minds. It's enough to encourage worship and thankfulness to Him!

- How have your pronouns changed in your thinking since you have been married? Is there less *me* and more *we*?
- Why is it easy to be content with physical expression of oneness and neglect working on oneness in other areas of your being?
- How is oneness different from sameness?
- What difference have you already noticed in the way each of you express sexual desire?

Prayer: Lord, your love and gifts to us are awesome. Thank you for the good gift of sexuality. Help us to experience the kind of blending of hearts and minds and purpose that you intend for us. Help us to be responsible and grateful, and to remember that you are pleased with our loving each other. Amen.

Reading 6

So God created human beings in his own image,
   in the image of God he created them;
   male and female he created them.
God blessed them and said to them, "Be fruitful and
   increase in number; fill the earth and subdue it" . . .
God saw all that he had made and it was very good.

GENESIS 1:27–28, 31

Then the Lord God formed a man from the dust of the ground and breathed into his nostrils the breath of life, and the man became a living being . . .

   So the Lord God caused the man to fall into a deep sleep; and while he was sleeping, he took one of the man's ribs . . . Then the Lord God made a woman from the rib he had taken out of the man.

GENESIS 2:7, 21–22

$\mathscr{I}$t's worth repeating that the Scripture clearly says that the image of God is both male and female—one humanity, two distinct persons. Equal, yet different. It takes both male and female to represent the image of God in the world. God gave His blessing to the man and the woman putting earth and its creatures in their care. Then He evaluated the culmination of His creation as *very good*.

The details of creation are brief, but profound in their implications. God fashioned the woman by removing a rib from the man. Her origin was not the same as that of the man. She is related to him in a significant way, but she is unique in creation, unmistakably her own person. She was taken out of man; the man surrendered part of himself to the making of the woman. He cannot separate himself from her, and neither can she isolate herself from him, for they are interdependent. It is God's doing—a mystery.

Adam's delight in finding a perfect counterpart and the subsequent union of Adam and Eve in marital partnership is God's completion of humanity. They became one flesh, modeling the unity within the Godhead. God called them Adam (mankind)—Mr. and Mrs. Adam, made in the image of God.

What an incredible beginning we have. This ineffable Creator God, full of love, stoops down to make human beings—male and female—in His image so they can enjoy each other. Then God walks and talks with them, letting himself be known.

- What new insights about your marriage do you have from looking afresh at God's creation of man and woman?
- If God still walked in the garden with you, as He did with Adam and Eve, what would you ask Him?
- What parts of being interdependent do you find difficult?

Prayer: Father, thank you for making each of us special in your sight and then bringing us together. Your love has blessed our love. Thank you that you still walk and talk with those who trust you and let yourself be known. Amen.

Reading 7

Then God said, "Let us make human beings in our image, in our likeness, so that they may rule over the fish in the sea and the birds in the sky, over the livestock and all the wild animals, and over all the creatures that move along the ground."

GENESIS 1:26

"'For in him we live and move and have our being.' As some of your own poets have said, 'We are his offspring.'"

ACTS 17:28

That you are made in God's image deserves even more thought. The implications are far-reaching for you and for your marriage. How would your daily life change if every morning you looked in the mirror and said, "I am made in the image of God"?

Since God is Spirit, not flesh and blood, you certainly don't bear a physical likeness. You already know you are not omniscient, omnipresent, and omnipotent. Thinking of God only in terms of the *omni* words—God's wisdom, infinitude, and power—can blind you to the wonder of being created in God's image. Then, in what ways are you like God?

First, **you are a rational being**. You have been created with the capacity to think, to reason. God himself is all intelligence, and our intelligence is grounded in His.

He made you a word-partner with himself so you can communicate—communicate with God and with each other. The use of language is a profound responsibility. You can communicate ideas and define goals and order priorities. You can think abstract thoughts and contemplate God and your own nature. You can reveal your inner self to others.

No other creature made by God has these gifts. They are yours because He made you a human being. God has no stereotypes of women and men in this regard.

Second, **you have creativity** because you are related to the ultimate Creator. Remember that the next time originality bursts upon you. This is not all that the "likeness to God" involves, but it is enough to think about for one day. There's more ahead.

- What is your response as you consider this rational likeness to God?
- How conscious are you that "being rational" makes you accountable to God in specific ways?
- How should your use of language reflect that you are in the image of God? (Ooh, that's a biggie!)

Prayer: Father God, we rarely thank you for being able to think and reason. What a gift to be able to use words to explain who we are to each other, to tell each other how we feel. You have, indeed, crowned us with glory and honor, and we thank you! Amen.

Reading 8

"And from each human being, too, I will demand an accounting for the life of another human being.

"Whoever sheds human blood,
by human beings shall their blood be shed;
for in the image of God
has God made humankind."

GENESIS 9:5–6

$\mathcal{G}$od said these words to Noah after the flood. They are a declaration of the importance of human beings in His sight. These words restate the honor God gives the human beings He created. He also affirms that the image of God in His creation was not destroyed by the disobedience of Adam and Eve (what we refer to as *the fall*).

Let's return to the question of what it means to be made in God's image to try to understand the immensity of this concept. It may sound academic to consider this, but it is no small thing to be created a human being.

You are created a moral person. This is a dignity God gave you. He has made you responsible for choices; you can choose. However, your choices affect not only your relationship with God, but with each other. Because you are a relational being, there is no such thing as a private choice. Your actions always affect other people.

You are created a spiritual person. You are physical, tied to the earth; yet you are spiritual, tied to heaven. You know intuitively that you are more than body. Your greatest longings lie in this part of your being. You are not autonomous, but dependent, and eternity is written on your heart.

You are created a relational person. Your sexuality—your bodily design that urges you toward each other—verifies your relational nature. People do not know themselves in isolation, but always in fellowship. Communion is what the image of God is about. You have a longing to be known. You can transcend yourself and tell each other who you are and how you feel.

- How does each of these gifts that reflect God's image affect your marriage?
- How do you treat someone who is made in God's image?
- Why is it wrong for either of you to hide behind silence in solving disagreements?

Prayer: L ORD *God, this is a big subject to think about. Help us to see each other as "made in your image" and rejoice at the special place we have in your world. Make our life together reflect your nature in the world in ways that bring honor to your name. Amen.*

Reading 9

*Now the serpent was more crafty than any of the wild animals the L*ORD *God had made. He said to the woman, "Did God really say, 'You must not eat from any tree in the garden'?"*

The woman said to the serpent, "We may eat fruit from the trees in the garden, but God did say, 'You must not eat fruit from the tree that is in the middle of the garden, and you must not touch it, or you will die.'"

"You will not certainly die," the serpent said to the woman. "For God knows that when you eat of it your eyes will be opened, and you will be like God, knowing good and evil."

GENESIS 3:1–5

$\mathcal{A}$ snake in Paradise. What a terrible reality.

No record is given of how long the man and woman lived in bliss together in Paradise. But however long it was, it was likely a life of both quantity and quality, fresh in the dew of God's creation.

God gave the man and the woman the world to enjoy, a garden to tend, full of good things, but He set one boundary, "the tree of the knowledge of good and evil." This boundary—this tree—the only limitation God gave, became the focal point of temptation.

The Tempter's approach to the woman was pious: he talked about God. In his crafty way, and by dangling an exaggeration before her, he began to sow seed of doubt in her mind about God's goodness. (*He is keeping something from you!*) He implied that she took God too seriously. (*Did God really mean that?*) Then the Serpent waited for the venom of his words to take effect.

$\mathcal{W}$HEN GOD WANTED TO SHOW US THE AWFUL REALITY OF SIN HE DID NOT BEGIN WITH A DEFINITION OF SIN. INSTEAD, HE TELLS US A STORY ABOUT THE WRONG CHOICES MADE BY A COUPLE LIVING IN PARADISE.

Only a free person can worship God and do His will. Inherent in freedom is the idea of having options, even the option to do wrong. Because we are creatures and not

Creator, we have boundaries to our freedom, boundaries that remind us from whom we receive that freedom.

Make a pact to remind each other about what is really important, to keep your eyes on God's goodness.

- What made the Serpent's approach so effective? Was it really about a tree?
- What evidence do you have that the Tempter hasn't changed his strategy in making people discontented?
- How can you help each other to focus on what you have instead of what you don't have?

Prayer: Creator God, keep our hearts and minds centered on you. To be discontented with what you provide seems an awful thing. Remind us daily to keep our focus on goodness and the truth of your Word. Amen.

Reading 10

When the woman saw that the fruit of the tree was good for food and pleasing to the eye, and also desirable for gaining wisdom, she took some and ate it. She also gave some to her husband, who was with her, and he ate it.

Then the eyes of both of them were opened, and they realized they were naked; so they sewed fig leaves together and made coverings for themselves.

GENESIS 3:6–7

The Serpent offered the woman attractive possibilities: to not die, to have her eyes opened, to know everything— to be like God.

What happened after the Serpent left the woman to think about their discussion? She began to focus on the prohibited tree. And the more she looked, the more desirable it became. Around her were "all kinds of trees... trees that were pleasing to the eye and good for food" (Genesis 2:9). She didn't lack anything. She certainly wasn't suffering from hunger. And she didn't talk it over with God.

> ALL SIN IS ROOTED IN UNBELIEF. WE DON'T TRUST THAT GOD CAN AND WILL HANDLE OUR LIVES FAIRLY AND WELL.
>
> — MARTIN LUTHER

She looked until she was consumed with desire. Just one piece of fruit. Try it out. (*God wants us to enjoy life here, doesn't He?*) And so she did what was forbidden. She ate, and gave some to her husband who was there with her. (*No one wants to sin alone!*) And their world fell apart. Everything changed.

The purity of their relationship was spoiled. What was supposed to be self-enhancing destroyed their togetherness. Suddenly they knew shame and tried to do a cover-up with fig leaves.

"Shame is the painful feeling that we are not the persons we ought to be: to be ashamed is to have a sense of our fractured lives, a longing to be whole." (Lewis Smedes)

The history of human beings falling from grace began with something very small and quiet.

"So simple an act, so hard its undoing. God will taste poverty and death before [Satan's] 'Take and eat' become verbs of salvation." (Derek Kidner)

Sin is a spoiler. Obedience is choosing God's best, no matter what any deceiver may say.

- How can you keep your daily focus on truth instead of pointlessly desiring something you don't have? Or wanting to be more than you are?
- In what ways is it right to feel that there is more to life than you are experiencing?
- What have you found is the secret to contentment? How does this affect obedience to God?

Prayer: Lord, the behavior and choice of Mr. and Mrs. Adam seem so stupid from our vantage point. It wasn't as if they needed more. Yet we suspect that temptations like this could easily trip us up, too. Keep us free from choices that destroy. We want to do your will. Amen.

Reading 11

Then the man and his wife heard the sound of the LORD God as he was walking in the garden in the cool of the day, and they hid from the LORD God among the trees of the garden. But the LORD God called to the man, "Where are you?"

He answered, "I heard you in the garden, and I was afraid because I was naked; so I hid."

And he said, "Who told you that you were naked? Have you eaten from the tree that I commanded you not to eat from?"

And the man said, "The woman you put here with me—she gave me some fruit from the tree, and I ate it."

Then the LORD God said to the woman, "What is this you have done?"

And the woman said, "The serpent deceived me, and I ate."
GENESIS 3:8–13

The bad news is that sin always makes us want to hide—from God and from each other. We don't like admitting we are wrong, so we hide, blame each other, or make excuses. God wants us to come out in the open and face up to our mistakes.

The good news is that God is always out there looking for us, calling "Where are you?" God knew where Adam was. But He wanted *Adam* to know where he was and face up to what he had done. God has a remedy for mistakes and wrong choices. From the very beginning it seems clear that God is in the business of restoring people to fellowship.

Wisdom tells you to keep short accounts with each other in the face of misunderstandings or wrongs done in marriage. But scared

> LOVE COVERS SIN, YET LOVE ALSO EXPOSES SIN. LOVE IS RESPONSIBLE; IT HAS AN ABIDING QUALITY. IT WILL NEVER BE TRANSFORMED INTO SOMETHING BETTER, FOR IT IS ITSELF THE TRANSFORMING POWER. LOVE BEGETS LOVE. LOVE KNOWS NO AGE LIMIT; LOVE NEVER ENDS.

humanness still wants to hide or blame. It's the difference between being open with each other or closed.

If you want a happy marriage (and life with God!) you will learn how to settle all misunderstandings and wrongs quickly. You have to stop wearing your own designer fig leaves. What have you to lose by admitting you were wrong?

Forgiveness is God's gracious gift of love to you. God is getting you ready for heaven where you will know perfection. But right now He wants you to start with honesty.

Marriage is full of opportunities to love and to extend grace to each other. Both of you are imperfect. When you keep on loving and extending grace, you are living out the image of God in you.

- What do you still need to learn about handling guilt?
- How can you keep from handling resentments in sneaky ways?
- How sure are you of God's forgiveness of your sins?

Prayer: Father God, thank you for calling out to find us wherever we are. Help us to be honest with you and with each other, unafraid to admit wrong and to ask forgiveness. Give us open faces and open hearts. Thanks that failure is not final with you. Amen.

Reading 12

Marriage should be honored by all, and the marriage bed kept pure, for God will judge the adulterer and all the sexually immoral. Keep your lives free from the love of money and be content with what you have, because God has said,

"Never will I leave you,
     never will I forsake you."

HEBREWS 13:4–5

Sex is a holy thing. Sex is God's idea. It is good. That's why together a husband and a wife can be physically naked with no shame. They can also be naked emotionally and be safe with each other. Yet these verses seem to indicate that your sexual relationship needs protection. It needs to be honored and kept pure.

Keeping the marriage bed pure means that you will make "a covenant with [your] eyes" (Job 31:1) to not look at anything that causes lustful thoughts—whether in person or on the page or screen. It means deciding that you will control your thought-life. Lust is encouraged and excused with jokes in our culture, but it is no joke. Lust is best defined as *a fire in the wall* of the house, bent on destroying it. In contrast, love is like an inviting fire on the hearth, offering comfort and pleasure. Lust uses other people to selfish ends. It does not build; it destroys.

The promise "to keep yourself for each other only" made in your wedding vows is a serious promise. This text gives fair warning that God judges adultery and immorality.

At first reading it seems strange that in two adjoining sentences these verses from Hebrews talk about sex and money. Maybe it is because these are two pitfalls in every marriage—pitfalls because of the temptation to think these are things we manage, almost as if God couldn't be expected to care about such earthy issues.

Not so. Whatever is valuable lends itself to counterfeits. God wants redeemed people to know the true delight of being sexual persons, to feel, to think, and to share, instead of being caged by unchosen or unworthy urges. In a materialistic world, He wants you to be free from a love of money that counterfeits true happiness. God wants to talk with you about every part of life, and to give you a holy freedom in these two areas that cause most marital disputes.

It's in the context of marriage and money and contentment that God reminds you that He will never leave you nor forsake you. Is there anything you can't discuss with Him?

- How do you feel about God not only being concerned about your sex life, but present in your love-making?
- What are the implications of His never leaving or forsaking you?
- How can you tell if you love money? What would analyzing your checkbook tell you about your financial priorities?

Prayer: Thanks, Lord God, for your practical love and care, for being with us in our most intimate moments. Keep us loving you, thankful for the true gifts, avoiding counterfeits that only make us discontented with what you have provided for us. Amen.

Reading 13

And this is my prayer: that your love may abound more and more in knowledge and depth of insight, so that you may be able to discern what is best and may be pure and blameless for the day of Christ, filled with the fruit of righteousness, that comes through Jesus Christ—to the glory and praise of God.

Philippians 1:9

Love abounding "in knowledge and depth of insight." Post these words in plain sight or in your heart as a goal for your marriage. The apostle Paul's prayer encompasses the whole of the Christian life, and certainly that includes marriage.

Love is a growing thing. You don't really *know* each other, even though you think you do. Living together will soon reveal that "oneness" is not sameness. You will increasingly find that, contrary to all the secular talk about gender sameness, men and women do not think alike. They are equal, yet different. That's not bad; that's good. But it will require that you listen to each other, that you develop "depth of insight" in a way that honors the other's uniqueness in God's sight.

> Love amazes us. It is at once an abstract idea, an experience, a virtue, and an action. It is a noun, yet it has no personal meaning unless it is a verb.

You have probably discovered by now that you respond differently to events and circumstances—that your values on the "little" things are not the same. Your concept of time and its wise use may differ. You may have different ways of doing almost everything! It is not likely that you will both "squeeze the toothpaste" in the same way. Some things that annoy are not good or bad; they may be the result of habits, family ways of doing things, or just plain thoughtlessness.

A good definition of love is that it "desires another person's highest good." Think about the implications of this. Love is no small task. Love will convince you to pray for "depth of insight" so that you can understand what the highest good is for another person and for your marriage.

Probably you will seem most lonely when you feel deeply about something that you have experienced, read, or felt—and your beloved doesn't get it! That's when you need to *discern* and listen and ask questions. That's an opportunity to grow "in knowledge and depth of insight." Easy? No. Necessary? Yes.

That's why you need to pray "that your love may abound more and more."

- What differences in your way of thinking come from "family values" that were instilled in you?
- How crucial are these in the bigger picture of a happy marriage?
- If these are issues that really matter, how can you help each other change?

Prayer: Lord, we want this prayer for the Philippians to be our prayer for ourselves. Make our love abound more and more in knowledge and depth of insight so that we may discern what is best—to the glory and praise of God. Amen.

*R*eading 14

*Wives, **in the same way** submit yourselves to your own husbands so that, if any of them do not believe the word, they may be won over without words by the behavior of their wives, when they see the purity and reverence of your lives. Your beauty should not come from outward adornment . . . it should be that of your inner self, the unfading beauty of a gentle and quiet spirit, which is of great worth in God's sight.*

1 PETER 3:1–4 (EMPHASIS ADDED)

*Husbands, **in the same way** be considerate as you live with your wives, and treat them with respect as the weaker partner and as heirs with you of the gracious gift of life, so that nothing will hinder your prayers.*

1 PETER 3:7 (EMPHASIS ADDED)

These verses from 1 Peter 3 come in the context of the apostle Peter urging all first-century Christians to have the kind of relationships that cause unbelievers to take notice. A lifestyle that glorifies God, he writes, shows proper respect for others (see 1 Peter 2:11–25). Peter uses the word "submit" in each relationship he mentions, including citizens toward government, and slaves toward masters. Probably the concept of "submitting" was not any more popular in the first century than it is now.

When he writes to husbands and wives, Peter urges them to demonstrate the gospel in daily life, to model their lifestyle after that of Jesus Christ, whose submission made Him willing to give himself by dying for us.

Submission is a good word; it is a Christian word. Our culture makes a negative of this word; it becomes a "doormat" concept. Sometimes examining the opposite meaning of a word (its antonym) helps clarify meaning. What is the opposite of a submissive attitude? The dictionary gives the words *resisting*, *fighting*, *stubborn*, *unyielding*—hardly words that make for peaceful relationships.

When Peter tells husbands and wives to submit to each other, he adds the phrase "in the same way," which refers directly to Christ's submission in giving His life. It's all about selfless love and gentleness on the part of both husbands and wives. Submission is not a one-sided responsibility, in which one person does all the submitting because the other person is always right.

How do husbands and wives submit? They show respect and consideration for each other. It's not simply an arbitrary rule laid on a marriage. Peter observes that husbands need to be aware of equality of persons, even though one may be weaker than the other; and wives need to return respect with a quiet and gentle spirit, concerned about the kind of beauty the Lord values. You are both "heirs together of the gracious gift of life," (NKJV) and to live without this kind of submissive attitude will hinder your prayers!

The verse that follows shows us what submission looks like in practice: "All of you, be like-minded, be sympathetic, love one another, be compassionate and humble" (1 Peter 3:8). It's a good thing in a marriage.

- What would keep you from being submissive to one another?
- What is there in your attitude toward "submission" that may need to be changed?
- What mental picture comes to your mind when you read the words: "heirs together of the gracious gift of life"?

Prayer: Heavenly Father, thank you for Christ's example of self-giving. We want to model our lives after His. Make us sensitive to issues of respect and honor for each other. We pray that love will reign in our home. For the glory of Christ, Amen.

Reading 15

The fruit of the Spirit is love, joy, peace, patience, kindness, goodness, faithfulness, gentleness and self-control.

GALATIANS 5:22

$\mathcal{W}$hat an impressive list of character traits! Who would not want these in their life? Read them over a second time. This list is a prescription for a good life and a good marriage.

How does a person develop these character traits? The text says they are the fruit of the Spirit. It's His fruit in you. These traits are not produced by self-effort. God cultivates them in your life as you obey Him, trust Him, and give Him rightful place in your life. And it is not fruits—but fruit. You don't get to pick and choose. They are so inter-related that you can't have one without the other.

However, the Spirit may zero in on different aspects of this fruit at different times in your life. After all, His business is to continually work in your life to make you conform more and more to the image of Christ.

For example, *self-control*, the last trait in the list, is a "biggie" that affects all of the other traits in the list. Self-control reinforces the idea of responsibility, the exercise of your will in cooperating with what the Spirit wants to do. "I just can't help myself"—the common cry heard today—is a rejection of responsibility. Contemporary culture believes that self-control is an impossible ideal. Not so; it is the fruit of the Spirit's work in you. He provides the nurture that helps you work this out in your character.

Because God wants to get you ready for heaven, as well as provide richness for this present life, the Spirit will be working on His fruit in your lives all your life. It's really what you want, so cooperate with Him and tell Him you want Him to do it!

- Pick out one characteristic of the "fruit" in the list and tell how you think this would look in your life together.
- Which trait do you find the most difficult? Which one will the Spirit likely make His target in your life?
- What can you do help each other in "fruit production"?

Prayer: God, forbid that we would claim to want you in our lives without wanting the fruit your presence produces. Remind us often of the Spirit's work and make us together more and more like Jesus. Amen.

Reading 16

Give thanks to the Lord, for he is good; his love endures forever.

PSALM 118:1

For although they knew God, they neither glorified him as God nor gave thanks to him, but their thinking became futile and their foolish hearts were darkened.

ROMANS 1:22

And be thankful.

COLOSSIANS 3:15

Thankfulness is a learned art. As you were growing up, you were *taught* to say "thank you" as a given response to kindnesses. Self-absorbed children don't naturally express appreciation. (Remember all those thank-you notes your mother made you write?)

Spontaneous thankfulness is a mark of spiritual maturity. Your expressions of thankfulness to those close to you (parents, siblings, friends) may accurately measure how thankful you are to God. Take inventory on this. Thankfulness comes from an overflowing heart.

The Bible is a handbook on thankfulness. The psalms are a litany of thanksgiving. The apostle Paul repeats the instruction in letter after letter, "And be thankful" (Colossians 3:15); "Give thanks in all circumstances" (1 Thessalonians 5:18). He writes, "I thank my God every time I remember you"

> LOVE IS SPECIFIC, NOT VAGUE. IT IS DISCERNING. LOVE KNOWS AND UNDERSTANDS. LOVE HAS A STANDARD.

(Philippians 1:3). Other times he bursts into a doxology: "Thanks be to God for his indescribable gift!" (2 Corinthians 9:15). Yet when he lists the deeds of the wicked, Paul singles out *thanklessness*: "They neither glorified him as God nor gave thanks to him" (Romans 1:21). Thanklessness seems like the last straw!

Thankfulness builds relationships. It reminds you of how much you owe to one another, and that you are not the center of the universe, deserving of all the goodness that surrounds your life. Spontaneous thankfulness to each other for small and large kindnesses is good for a marriage.

And don't forget to thank God for mercy after mercy in your life—things both small and great. Thankfulness reminds you of who you are and who God is, which is a good reality check.

- Why is thankfulness so important?
- What does it do in your own life? What does it do for the recipient of your thankfulness?
- Why is lack of thankfulness, particularly to God, such a serious thing?

Prayer: Lord, it's hard to be thankful enough for all you've given us. Teach us how to express specific prayers of thankfulness so that we will be reminded of your grace in our lives. Keep us from vague asking and vague thanking—for our own good and your glory. Amen.

Reading 17

"Therefore I tell you, do not worry about your life, what you will eat or drink; or about your body, what you will wear. Is not life more important than food, and the body more important than clothes? Look at the birds of the air; they do not sow or reap or store away in barns, and yet your heavenly Father feeds them. Are you not more valuable than they? Can any one of you by worrying add a single hour to your life?

"And why do your worry about clothes? See how the flowers of the field grow. They do not labor or spin. Yet I tell you that not even Solomon in all his splendor was dressed like one of these. If that is how God clothes the grass of the field, which is here today and tomorrow is thrown into the fire, will he not much more clothe you—you of little faith? So do not worry, saying, 'What shall we eat?' or 'What shall we drink?' or 'What shall we wear?' For the pagans run after all these things, and your heavenly Father knows that you need them. But seek first his kingdom and his righteousness, and all these things will be given to you as well. Therefore do not worry about tomorrow, for tomorrow will worry about itself. Each day has enough trouble of its own."

THE WORDS OF JESUS IN MATTHEW 6:25–34

*E*xpect material difficulties in this world. You have everything carefully budgeted, and just enough money to pay all the bills—and then an expensive and unexpected crisis hits you. It leaves a worry-sized pain in your stomach. Worry hovers over you. What will you do?

This Scripture tells you not to worry. How is this possible? Ask the birds of the air, Jesus says. Check out what the wild flowers tell you. God's unfailing faithfulness answers the question. He knows the specifics of your situation. "Your heavenly Father knows," Jesus tells us. And Peter wrote, "Cast all your anxiety on him because he cares for you" (1 Peter 5:7).

Trusting God does not eliminate your need to plan wisely, tighten your belt, or change your priorities. It just acknowledges that God knows your situation and that you can look to Him for a solution. In the middle of trouble, trusting encourages you to sing a hymn of praise about God's faithfulness.

Jesus' second instruction is to make sure your priorities are right. Are you seeking God's kingdom, pursuing righteousness? If so, His promise is that "all these things will be given you as well." You are in on something bigger than material well-being—something that involves eternity. Why worry when you can trust?

- Which is harder—worrying how you will do it or trusting God? Why is trusting God so hard?
- One of you may be a natural "worrier." How can you help each other without seeming to give easy platitudes?
- What planning do you need to do to keep your life orderly? Do you have a budget?

Prayer: Lord, thank you for reminding us that you are our Father, that you not only know about our anxieties but you also care. Help us to seek your kingdom and your righteousness. Make us wise in our material decisions, and keep our focus on loving and living for you. Thank you. Amen.

Reading 18

"Ask and it will be given to you; seek and you will find; knock and the door will be opened to you. For everyone who asks receives; those who seek find; and to those who knock, the door will be opened.

"Which of you, if your son asks for bread, will give him a stone? Or if he asks for a fish, will give him a snake? If you, then, though you are evil, know how to give good gifts to your children, how much more will your Father in heaven give good gifts to those who ask him! So in everything, do to others what you would have them do to you, for this sums up the Law and the Prophets."

THE WORDS OF JESUS IN MATTHEW 7:7–12.

$\mathcal{G}$od is your Father, and He gives only good gifts to His children. Jesus makes it clear in this illustration in Matthew that the Father's goodness and generosity far exceed your own.

Jesus also gives a lesson in prayer. As He prepares to return to heaven and leave His disciples, He reminds them to *ask* for what they need. Why does He want them to ask? Because, as James later warns, "You do not have because you do not ask God. When you ask, you do not receive, because you ask with wrong motives, that you may spend what you get on your pleasures" (James 4:2–3). This is true for you, too.

The verb order in verses 7 and 8 is interesting: *ask, seek, knock.* Why does *seeking* come between *asking* and *knocking*? *Seeking* is there as a reminder that you need to find out if the *asking* prayer is sensitive to God's will. *Asking* prayers can be selfish. Seeking means that you take time to evaluate your motives.

Knocking prayers are about persistence, but why persist if you have confidence about God's will? Some people question why we are urged to pray if God knows our needs anyway. How would you answer that? What does asking, seeking, and knocking teach you about your relationship to God?

Jesus concludes with an interesting last sentence. Read it again and you will find that it is the Golden Rule, and at first glance it seems out of place in the context. But maybe Jesus is saying, "Prayer should not only make you sensitive to God's will. God is sensitive to your needs; and you need to have that same sensitivity to the needs of others." Prayer is as much about giving as it is about receiving.

- What have you discovered about yourself in this business of asking, seeking, and knocking?
- Why does God want us to ask?
- How does the way we pray tell us what we really believe about prayer?

Prayer: Lord Jesus, teach us how to pray. Keep us from making our prayers vain repetitions and cavalier requests. It is awesome that you allow us to come into your presence to ask, seek, and knock. Give us a strong sense of talking to a Real Person about real needs as we come to you. Amen.

Reading 19

[Speak] to one another with psalms, hymns and songs from the Spirit. Sing and make music from your heart to the Lord, always giving thanks to God the Father for everything, in the name of our Lord Jesus Christ.

EPHESIANS 5:19–20

It's an old saying, "He who sings prays twice." Singing is important to God. He created music. Your voices are His gift and He put songs in your hearts. Don't miss the sheer joy of singing together as husband and wife.

Singing is a particularly Christian habit. It is mentioned in the Bible over and over. The morning stars sang together at the creation of the earth. Whenever there was a victory for the people of Israel they sang a new song. Psalms is a biblical hymnal. Down through the years saints of God have been composing songs and singing their faith.

Why not sing a hymn with these readings? Get used to singing together on the golden days so that you can sing together on the cloudy days. Expand your hymnody, your repertoire of songs. Be a singing family from the first days of your life together. Sing as you drive along in the car. Include lighthearted songs from the secular world, or songs you learned at camp. It's a good way to enjoy each other and the world God has made for your pleasure. Joy is one of His gifts.

Many times throughout our life when we were faced with disappointments or serious decisions, or uncertainty about what to do next, one of us would begin singing a hymn and the other would join in. We found that as we sang, great truths about God lifted our spirits, bringing renewed trust and fresh commitment. That's one reason to keep a hymnal in your car and near your dining table. A good hymn has a way of expanding your heart.

Christians have a lot to sing about. Joy should bubble up in song as you live together. Make sure that it does. A song-less home seems an empty place.

- Talk about favorite songs from you childhood and how you feel about singing.
- Did you grow up in a singing household? Do you want your own home to be a singing household?
- Our world is full of iPods and canned music. Why does singing together yourselves create a better environment than this?

Prayer: Lord, put a song in our hearts! Help us to express our faith, our love, and our courage in songs and hymns and spiritual songs. May this not only give us joy, but also be a witness to an often song-less world. Thank you for giving us so much to sing about. Amen.

P.S. Why not sing a favorite hymn right now?

Reading 20

We know and rely on the love God has for us. God is love. Whoever lives in love lives in God, and God in them.

There is no fear in love. But perfect love drives out fear, because fear has to do with punishment. The one who fears is not made perfect in love. We love because he first loved us.

1 JOHN 4:16, 18–19

Can you affirm that the first sentence in today's reading is true in your life? It strikes us as being a HUGE statement. Whatever we know about love we learn from God. He IS love. We love because He loves us.

Yet how incredibly careless we are with that word *love*. We say we love lemon pie and sports cars, and in the next breath say we love each other and we love God.

God is not so fickle or careless. His love is a commitment, not a passing fancy. His love purposes to untangle and unclutter our lives and free us to be all He had in mind when He created us. He accepts us as we are, forgives us,

Love acts; it is not simply a sentiment.

gives us eternal life, and then begins the practical work of bringing us into His highest good. It's a good thing to know and rely on that.

Here's a repeat of a definition of love we mentioned before: *Love is desiring another's highest good.* Another definition is similar, but has an added dimension: *Love creates for another person the environment that enables that person to become all that God has in mind.* Do either of these concepts define the love you have for each other?

The idea of creating an environment where persons grow and thrive is exciting and stretches the imagination. Together you are establishing just such a place—a home.

What an emotionally evocative word *home* is! Home is a safe place. It is the place where you belong, where you are accepted for who you are, and where those who love you want to work in cooperation with God to make your life fulfilling. There is no fear in an environment that is a safe place. God's love provides that for us; and He wants us to provide it for each other.

- What can you do to assure that your home is a safe place?
- How will love change the environment of your home?
- Do you feel safe in your home?

Prayer: Father God, we bring our life before you with thankfulness for the love shown to us in the Lord Jesus Christ. Take our lives and teach us how to love each other. May the overflow of our love create a climate of encouragement in our home that reaches out to others. For your glory and our good. Amen.

Reading 21

We who are strong ought to bear with the failings of the weak and not to please ourselves. We should all please our neighbors for their good, to build them up . . . May the God who gives endurance and encouragement give you the same attitude of mind toward each other that Christ Jesus had, so that with one mind and voice you may glorify the God and Father of our Lord Jesus Christ. Accept one another, then, just as Christ accepted you, in order to bring praise to God.

ROMANS 15:1–2, 5–7

Carry each other's burdens, and in this way you will fulfill the law of Christ. If any of you think you are something when you are nothing, you deceive yourselves. Each of you should test your own actions. Then you can take pride in yourself, without comparing yourself to somebody else, for each of you should carry your own load.

GALATIANS 6:2–5

While these Scripture passages, so rich in content, were written to believers in the churches at Rome and Galatia, they contain principles relevant to your marriage.

You already know that you have different strengths and weaknesses, different personalities. While you may need to change and to grow, your natural gifts differ. Thus, you need to be sensitive to each other's weaknesses, even though you may dislike the idea of someone else "bearing with your failings."

Love—the love we read and talked about in the previous reading—reminds you that you are not the center of the universe and that your goal is not "to please yourself" but to build a good working relationship and support each other. The reminder that God gives you endurance and encouragement will help you in working out the small stuff that causes irritations. Love stops petty quarrels and nagging.

Accept one another and grow together in His grace. Your goal is unity in following Christ, so talk about your differences. Don't internalize irritation or annoyance or anger; don't shut the other person out with the silent treatment (which makes home unsafe!) Remember that Christ accepted you just as you were.

The second passage from Galatians seems to contradict itself. First it tells you to carry one another's burdens, and ends with the suggestion that each person is to carry his or her own load.

- What do you think this passage is saying about helping each other?
- What is saying about taking responsibility for our own life?
- Why is it important to have a realistic view of your own strengths and weaknesses?

Prayer: Holy Spirit, teach us how to support and encourage each other in a way that honors the God-given difference in our personalities. Thank you that you are the source of both encouragement and endurance. Amen.

Reading 22

Trust in the Lord with all your heart
*   and lean not on you own understanding;*
in all your ways submit to him,
*   and he will make your paths straight.*

PROVERBS 3:5–6

You will keep in perfect peace
*   those whose minds are steadfast,*
*   because they trust in you.*
Trust in the Lord forever,
*   for the LORD, the LORD, is the Rock eternal.*

ISAIAH 26:3–4

Trusting God is what the Christian life is really all about. It's the opposite of fear. Fear either paralyzes you or causes you to rush in and take matters into your own hands. Trust lets God be in charge, talks issues over with the Father, and *rests* in Him.

Trust is not a magic talisman that you wear around your neck. It is not superstition or wishful thinking. It is not blind faith that has no substance. No leap in the dark here. Trust is a certainty because of WHO we are trusting.

Personal trust in God is a cord made up of three strands: knowledge, humility, and an obedient attitude.

Knowledge is essential because you need to know who God is, what He is like, and what He has done in human history. You usually don't trust someone you don't know. That's why Bible study is so important; it keeps expanding your knowledge of God.

Humility means that you do not think you know more than God. Humility lets God be God and remembers that His ways are higher than your ways, and His thoughts higher than your thoughts (Isaiah 55:9).

An *obedient attitude* means that you recognize that life offers you choices, and those choices have moral significance. Life offers many options and some of those options can seem very attractive. The test for an obedient heart usually comes when the pressure is on.

Trust goes beyond feelings or fear; it brings God's redemption to every part of life. All relationships are built on trust. Your relationship with God began that way, and it flourishes and grows as you persist in trusting. Remember Aslan, the golden-maned lion of Narnia, once said to Lucy, "Every year you grow you will find me bigger." (*Prince Caspian* by C. S. Lewis.)

- How will your trust in God affect your trust in each other?
- Which of the three strands of the cord keeps you from trusting God more fully?
- When you look back over your life, in what ways has your trust in God grown?

Prayer: LORD God, help our faith to be growing—growing in knowledge, in humility, and in obedience to you. Forgive us for the times when we talk or act as if you were our last hope rather than our first! No one who has trusted in you has ever been sorry. Fasten our hopes on you—the LORD God who is our rock. Amen.

Reading 23

I urge you, brothers and sisters, in view of God's mercy, to offer your bodies as a living sacrifice, holy and pleasing to God—this is true worship. Do not conform to the pattern of this world, but be transformed by the renewing of your mind. Then you will be able to test and approve what God's will is—his good, pleasing and perfect will.

ROMANS 12:1–2

Then we will no longer be infants, tossed back and forth by the waves, and blown here and there by every wind of teaching and by the cunning craftiness of people in their deceitful scheming. Instead, speaking the truth in love, we will in all things grow up into him who is the head, that is, Christ.

EPHESIANS 4:14–15

God has more in mind in bringing you together than making you happy. Happiness is always a by-product, never a goal.

Does it seem too unromantic to suggest that you need to talk about goals for your marriage? If you don't have some direction, you will simply let life happen to you.

How can you avoid "conforming to the pattern of this world"? What does a useful life look like? What are you aiming at? How flexible would you be if God asked you to leave a comfortable life to do something that seems less comfortable? Could you offer yourself sacrificially?

TRUTH IS LOVE'S COMPANION; IT KEEPS LOVE HONEST. BUT LOVE, IN TURN, SOFTENS TRUTH.

These are not rhetorical questions. They require answers, and the answers are bedrock on which to build your home. Creating a home where people feel the presence of God is no small thing. The way you live together will say something about God's truth. It will be a proclamation of your beliefs, whether you realize it or not.

Stability counts. but so does consistency. The Ephesians text mentions "speaking the truth in love" as a way to grow up in Christ. What does this mean for your relationship and the home you are creating?

And when it comes to the by-product of happiness in your marriage, much of your future happiness will come from looking back over years of living together and seeing green shoots of personal growth. Having goals gives focus to your life and helps you grow.

- Why does it matter to God that you two have come together to create a home?
- Discuss what you think a useful life together should look like.
- What do you want your marriage to say to the world about God?

Prayer: Lord, these verses are full of strong ideas. Help us to be open and honest in setting goals and finding out what you want to do in us and through us. Give us a life together that counts in terms of eternity. Amen.

Reading 24

Keep on loving one another as brothers and sisters. Do not forget to show hospitality to strangers, for by so doing some people have shown hospitality to angels without knowing it.

HEBREWS 13:1–2

Offer hospitality to one another without grumbling. Each of you should use whatever gift you have received to serve others, as faithful stewards of God's grace in its various forms.

1 PETER 4:9–10

$\mathcal{G}$od is hospitable. He welcomes you into His presence whenever you show up. He embraces and listens to you. He wants His children to be like Him in this.

People often find two excuses for not being hospitable. A newly married couple may be waiting for all the furnishings they think necessary for entertaining. Later, when they own a larger house and lots of stuff, they seldom invite anyone in because they don't have time.

An open heart always makes an open home. It's an inner attitude that says "I don't care about things or time; I care about you." You share what you have, not what you wish you had. You show love with a generous and welcoming heart. Jesus said when you do this to the "least" of these, you do it to Him.

Years ago we had a blue and white kitchen done in Dutch décor. On the soffit above the kitchen table

$\mathcal{L}$OVE IS INCREDIBLY STRETCHY. IT IS THE ROOMIEST OF ALL THE VIRTUES; THERE IS ALWAYS ROOM FOR ONE MORE PERSON.

we painted, in Dutch: "Stewards of God's manifold grace" (1 Peter 4:10). The words needed to be translated for most of our guests, and this gave us many opportunities to talk about God's grace with our guests. Around that kitchen table we served simple meals to people who made our lives rich with conversations and ideas. We likely entertained some angels unaware, since there are no "ordinary" people in God's world.

Over the years, in each of our homes, we have tried to display some words that speak of our faith, on the wall or elsewhere. This offers guests an opportunity to ask a question and gives us the privilege of answering the query. It's like flying the flag.

There is something profoundly Christian or sacred about gathering around the table, enjoying well-prepared food and good conversations. Even the Lord's Supper is called Communion because of what takes place around the table. You say something about your view of family life, your view of God and His provisions by the way you eat together.

"'Tis a gift to be simple, 'tis a gift to be free"—words from a folksong—are the key. You share what you have, not what you wish you had. Whatever that is, you show love with a welcoming heart. Jesus said when you do this to "the least of these," you do it to Him.

- How can you make "showing hospitality" a bigger part of your life?
- Someone once said that there are two kinds of people: givers and takers. Which do you want to be?
- Why do you think hospitality is an important Christian virtue?

Prayer: Heavenly Father, thank you for your hospitality to us! Help us to be like you in this. Take our lives, our home—whatever we have—and use it for your glory. All that we are and own you have given to us. May our generosity to others be part of our witness to your goodness. Amen.

Reading 25

Therefore each of you must put off falsehood and speak truthfully to your neighbor, for we are all members of one body.

"In your anger do not sin": Do not let the sun go down while you are still angry, and do not give the devil a foothold.

Those who have been stealing must steal no longer, but must work, doing something useful with their own hands, that they may have something to share with those in need.

EPHESIANS 4:25–28

The apostle Paul often repeats the phrase *one another* to emphasize that "we are members of one body," we belong to each other. Here he inspires Christians to consider how to live a life worthy of the Lord—a good life. Both of the issues he writes about affect *one another*; they are actions that either build or destroy oneness.

The first issue is *honesty*. Lies destroy trust, which in turn, destroys oneness. It's hard to belong to someone you can't trust. But he goes beyond lies to the positive, "tell the truth." Silence can sometimes be a lie. It can also be a way to hurt someone. Some things need to be said to enhance unity. Speak truthfully. Only cowards hide behind inappropriate silence. Remember that earlier in this letter he says believers should be "speaking the truth in love."

The second issue is *anger*. People do get angry. Jesus got angry at times. Anger is an honest human emotion. It is what you do with anger that matters. Don't let your anger lead to sin. Unchecked anger leads to destructive words and actions. It's best to examine why you are angry. Was it because a wrong or an injustice was done? Or because your expectations were not met? Are you accumulating irritations instead of handling them? Is it all about you, or the other person?

Whatever the reason, you are a rational person. Figure it out, and then settle things quickly, so that you don't give the devil a foothold in your lives. Do it before the sun goes down! Keep short accounts with grievances if you want a happy marriage.

The verses about stealing may seem irrelevant, but there are many ways to steal—stealing time that should belong to someone else, keeping something for yourself when you should be sharing, not doing your part.

Paul is giving inspired instruction about living a useful life so that you have something to invest in the life of someone else.

- Which of these practical instructions are hardest for you?
- What part does love play in each of these instructions?
- How does defensiveness or blaming shut down each of these instructions and destroy the quality of your life together?

Prayer: Thanks, Father, for your grace in making us your dearly loved children. Help us to walk in the way of love and take seriously these solemn instructions that lead to oneness of spirit and a healthy relationship. Thank you for the work of the Holy Spirit who nourishes us and produces His fruit in our lives. Teach us especially about discipline and self-control. Amen.

Reading 26

Do not let any unwholesome talk come out of your mouths, but only what is helpful for building others up according to their needs, that it may benefit those who listen.

And do not grieve the Holy Spirit of God, with whom you were sealed for the day of redemption. Get rid of all bitterness, rage and anger, brawling and slander, along with every form of malice.

Be kind and compassionate to one another, forgiving each other, just as in Christ God forgave you.

EPHESIANS 4:29–32

*W*atch your words. Unwholesome words come in many varieties. Some of them cut more deeply than sticks and stones. Some may be bitter, slanderous, full of malice and anger. Some are inappropriate—obscenity, foolish talk, or coarse joking. Some are false—a kind of manipulation to get what you want. Unwholesome words are hard to take back. They keep hanging around in our heads and hurting us.

Language is a gift, and words should be used to build others up. "Let your conversation be always full of grace, seasoned with salt" (Colossians 4:6). If you have been the recipient of gracious, healing words, even words seasoned with salt, then you know the value of kind words, compassionate words, forgiving words—words that make you a better person.

*L*OVE IS KIND, BUT ALL KINDNESS IS NOT LOVE. LOVE IS NOT SOFT; IT INSISTS ON WHAT IS RIGHT. IT ISN'T LOVE BECAUSE WE CALL IT LOVE.

Sometimes silence is appropriate, but in some situations silence can be evidence of a lack of compassion or kindness. The gift of language requires responsibility and spiritual discernment. To not say something that has the potential to encourage another person is a breach of kindness. Wholesome words, however, are also truthful words. Don't grieve the Holy Spirit with your words.

Forgiveness, according to this passage, is a result of kindness and compassion. God in Christ has forgiven you; as hard as it may be, then, on what basis can you avoid forgiving someone else? Forgiveness takes effort. God knows it is hard; it cost His Son's life. But when we forgive, we follow God's example as dearly loved children.

Forgive each other with His kind of generosity so your heart will be free. And don't be surprised if you find many occasions to practice this in your life together. This will make you extra thankful for God's grace.

- How do you feel about this instruction: *As Christ has been to me, so I must be to you.* Does it fit what the Scripture is saying?
- Share a time when the words of another person cheered your heart and set you on a good path. Talk about a time when you received an unkind or cutting comment and how it affected you.
- Why do some jests or jokes hurt so much?

Prayer: Thank you, Lord Jesus, for saving us from ourselves. Keep us clean both in our actions and in our words. Help us to be kind, compassionate, and forgiving to each other. Help us to be quick to apologize and ask forgiveness for words wrongly spoken. Season our lives with your grace. For our good and your glory. Amen.

Reading 27

Do not store up for yourselves treasures on earth, where moth and rust destroy, and where thieves break in and steal. But store up for yourselves treasures in heaven, where moth and rust do not destroy, and where thieves do not break in or steal. For where your treasure is, there your heart will be also . . .

No one can serve two masters. Either you will hate the one and love the other, or you will be devoted to the one and despise the other. You cannot serve both God and Money.

MATTHEW 6:19–21, 24

Godliness with contentment is great gain. For we brought nothing into the world, and we can take nothing out of it. But if we have food and clothing, we will be content with that . . .

For the love of money is a root of all kinds of evil. Some people, eager for money, have wandered from the faith and pierced themselves with many griefs.

But you . . . pursue righteousness, godliness, faith, love, endurance and gentleness.

1 TIMOTHY 6:6–8, 10–11

Remember the parable Jesus told about Mr. Bigger Barns who reveled in his wealth and kept building bigger and bigger barns to store all he owned? Jesus called him a fool—not because he was rich, but because he was not rich toward God. The problem was not how much the man had, but where his treasure really was. Where was his heart?

Treasure on earth has a way of blinding people to heavenly realities. Advertising entices you to want more than you need. What is a luxury for one becomes a necessity for another, which makes you judge another and excuse yourselves. It's a matter of values. Worldly logic will push you to choose more rather than less. A credit card makes this logic possible.

Throughout your life you need to be taking an inventory of your heart. Where is your treasure? That's where the true center of your life will be.

Sometimes parents can be your worst enemy when it comes to focusing on riches. We've seen parents load their children down with things they didn't know they "needed" or hardly wanted. Honest words may be necessary. "Don't let the world around you squeeze you into its own mould" (Romans 12:2, J. B. Phillips).

Things are not the source of either happiness or contentment. You are wise if you understand and believe this, and live by this truth from the beginning of your life together.

Probably more marital quarrels are over money than any other issues. The words "Be content with what you have" are wonderfully freeing, lest you find your confidence and well-being in things rather than God.

- How can you keep track of where your treasure is?
- How can you tell if you are rich toward God?
- "Give me neither poverty nor riches, but give me only my daily bread. Otherwise, I may have too much and disown you and say, 'Who is the Lord?' or I may become poor and steal, and so dishonor the name of my God" (Proverbs 30:8–9). Talk together about the wisdom in this proverb.

Prayer: Lord, help us to keep our balance in a materialistic world. Protect us from such poverty that we are consumed by financial needs. Protect us also from such plenty that we forget God and act as if we had earned pleasure for ourselves without regard to God. Give us heaven-rich hearts. Amen.

Reading 28

The husband should fulfill his marital duty to his wife, and likewise the wife to her husband. The wife does not have authority over her own body but yields it to her husband. In the same way, the husband does not have authority over his own body but yields it to his wife.

Do not deprive each other except perhaps by mutual consent and for a time, so that you may devote yourselves to prayer. Then come together again so that Satan will not tempt you because of your lack of self-control.

1 CORINTHIANS 7:3–5

$\mathcal{S}$ex is not a weapon. Sex is God's good idea for expressing marital oneness, for relaxing our bodies, for giving us joy. We seem to need reminding that sex is not something that we discovered, but a gift of God.

When sex becomes selfish or demanding, however, or is denied for invalid reasons, the sexual part of marriage is in trouble—a trouble that will threaten your oneness.

Look at those attitude words in the previous paragraph: *selfish*, *demanding*, and *denied*. There is little place, if any, for romance in any one of them, nor do they indicate a consciousness that God is in on this part of your life. They are "me" words, not "us" words.

Does God ask us to bring to our sexual life the same kind of tenderness, compassion, and understanding that He wants in the rest of our lives? Of course.

How practical God is to give instructions like these through the apostle Paul, a fellow who personally thought it was better to remain unmarried (1 Corinthians 7:7). If God can be this open about sexual issues, you should learn to be open, too. There is a lot to talk about in your sexual relationship—like a discussion of what pleases and what doesn't. After all, this is an act you do together, meant to be a delight for both.

There is a playful aspect to the sexual act, a leisurely discovering of each other and a necessary wooing that is important. This is not performance on demand; it is an expression of belonging to each other. It's appropriate to laugh at some of your predicaments. And always declare your love verbally as well as physically.

God is not so purposeful that He doesn't take time for joy. And neither should you be. God is pleased by a joyful, thankful heart. So let your sexual life be this in His sight. You may need to change your concept of God and of sex to make this a reality in your lives. But He is open to have you talk to Him about this.

- Is there anything about your life that God doesn't know about? If not, why are you embarrassed to think of God in connection with your lovemaking?
- What do you do when you know you have been insensitive to the other person?
- "Don't say with your actions more than you are prepared to say with your words," is good advice to consider. How do you respond to this wisdom?

Prayer: Creator God, our Maker, thank you for this gift of sexuality. Give us freedom and joy in our love for each other. Help us to see the sacred side of this, as well as the playful side, and to take this from your hand as your gift to us. Amen.

Reading 29

"Haven't you read," [Jesus] replied, "that at the beginning the Creator 'made them male and female,' and said 'For this reason a man will leave his father and mother and be united to his wife, and the two will become one flesh'? So they are no longer two, but one. Therefore what God has joined together, let no one separate."

"Why then," they asked, "did Moses command that a man give his wife a certificate of divorce and send her away?"

Jesus replied, "Moses permitted you to divorce your wives because your hearts were hard. But it was not this way from the beginning. I tell you that anyone who divorces his wife, except for sexual immorality, and marries another woman commits adultery."

MATTHEW 19:4–9

The Lord is the witness between you and the wife of your youth. You have been unfaithful to her, though she is your partner, the wife of your marriage covenant.

Has not the Lord made the two of you one? You belong to him in body and spirit. And why has he made you one? Because he was seeking godly offspring. So be on your guard, and do not be unfaithful to the wife of your youth.

"I hate divorce," says the Lord God.

MALACHI 2:14–16

$\mathcal{A}$s newly married, these verses may seem irrelevant, but they are not. They underscore the importance of your relationship in God's sight. Can you see evidence in these two biblical texts that your marriage was marked in heaven by the living God? It's a recorded covenant. You may think you got married, but what was God's part in it?

When a relationship is troubled, too often divorce becomes a first option. People who have not been paying attention to life suddenly feel competent to make a decision that denies all they earlier claimed to be true. Scripture makes it clear that a broken relationship is not God's highest good for a marriage or the people in it. He takes seriously the promises we make to each other.

You can always find reasons for trouble in a marriage, but none of them take God by surprise. He is the great problem-solver, but you have to go to Him and ask, and repent, and be open to His thoughts on solutions. He specializes in softening hearts.

Trouble comes from neglect in relationships. Husbands and wives take each other for granted. They stop sharing their dreams and assurances of love. They allow the urgent to push out the important. They stop talking to God and each other about things that matter. Make a promise to help each other keep priorities straight.

One of the reasons God hates divorce is the way it affects the next generation. God desires godly offspring (Malachi 2:15). Children are part of God's plan. Clearly when God puts two people together and makes them one, He has long-range plans in mind for a family—and every person in it. He wants to make everyone in the family "godly."

- What is your marriage covenant with each other?
- What are you learning together about the importance of conversations about values and truth?
- Do you know an older couple whose marriage models what you want to see in your own? What are you learning from them?

Prayer: Thank you, heavenly Father, for marrying us to each other, for making us one in body and spirit. Protect our love with your gracious presence, and remind us often that we are yours. Amen.

Reading 30

A cheerful heart is good medicine.

PROVERBS 17:22

There is a time for everything . . .
    a time to weep and a time to laugh.

ECCLESIASTES 3:1, 4

The Lord has done great things for us,
    and we are filled with joy.

PSALM 126:3

$\mathcal{G}$od has a sense of humor. Look at the animals He made: giraffes, hippos, camels, moose! What a combination of creativity and humor. And notice what He has done with two eyes, two ears, a nose and a mouth, making every human being look different.

Life can sometimes be too somber. Blessed is the couple who can laugh easily together. Humor is a gift, and it often can defuse what seems annoying and yet is relatively unimportant. It helps you not to sweat the small stuff of life. At least one of you needs to remember to see the funny side of events that might otherwise appear more weighty than they really are. Laughter is good medicine.

Have you ever thought about why God made people able to laugh? What a gift! "Joy," wrote C. S. Lewis, "is the serious business of heaven!" Why not make it the serious business of earth, too, whenever you can? It's possible to take yourself too seriously. You already know you are not perfect, and that some things in life just won't turn out right. Like a fallen cake or a disastrous fix-it job. How serious will it be in ten years' time? (But remember, there is an important difference between laughing *with* someone and laughing *at* someone.)

In His Sermon on the Mount, Jesus said that each day brings enough trouble of its own. Don't add to the problem by failing to see how ironic or funny many things in life really are. There is enough to make you weep in the world, so do everything you can to make your life together a full-cup, not a half-empty one. A good portion of joy is having the right perspective and being optimistic about the future.

We can wish you nothing better than that you will be eager followers of Jesus Christ, that you will love each other wisely and tenderly, and that you will enjoy the world and even its perplexities with hope and humor.

- Insecure people often use humor as a way of putting someone else down. How can you avoid that in your relationship?
- Evaluate yourselves in this matter of being able to laugh. Are you pretty evenly balanced?
- What's the difference between a cheerful heart and a careless heart?

Prayer: Lord God, the source of all our life, the hope of our future, our comfort in times of trouble, the giver of every good and perfect gift, furnish our life together with your kind of joy and laughter. For our good and your glory. Amen.

$\mathcal{N}$ow that you have finished thirty days of readings together, we hope you found it so profitable that you will make using the Scripture and talking about Truth a habit in your marriage.

Many of these ideas will become increasingly relevant as you add years to your marriage. We suggest that you plan to go through the readings in another year, and then two years later, and maybe even again after that. Sometimes the importance of an idea needs some life experience to understand it fully. As for the questions at the end of each reading, in a year or two you may find that you have different answers.

Keep on loving each other!

Note to the Reader

The publisher invites you to share your response to the message of this book by writing Discovery House Publishers, P.O. Box 3566, Grand Rapids, MI 49501, U.S.A. For information about other Discovery House books, music, videos, or DVDs, contact us at the same address or call 1-800-653-8333. Find us on the Internet at http://www.dhp.org/ or send an e-mail to books@dhp.org.